Sonnets

Sonnets of Life Well Spent
Copyright ©2012 Stanley Paul Thompson

ISBN: 978-0-9854153-6-5
Publisher: Mercury HeartLink
Printed in the United States of America

Book design by Mercury HeartLink
www.heartlink.com

All rights reserved. This book, or sections of this book, may not be reproduced or transmitted in any form without permission from the author.

Permission is granted to educators to create copies of individual poems for classroom or workshop assignments.

Contact Stanley Thompson at: stan@shellmonster.com

Sonnets

of Life Well Spent

Stanley Paul Thompson

Contents

ACKNOWLEDGMENTS

INTRODUCTION

DEDICATION

1 Let's Not Be Coy

FIRST SECTION

4   Steno Tablet
5   Lay Forth Your Poems
6   Little Comfort Felt in Wishful Thinking
7   Fervent Passion
8   Washed Then Away These Hurts
9   Some Say He Flew Away
10 Listen
11 Escape in Thought
12 The Task So Hard
13 My Three Poems Tonight
14 Sometimes I Feel Mauldin
15 That's a Job for Goblins
16 Let Me Dream This Tonight
17 Will of the Gods

18	Time Wasted in Rhyme
19	Welcome the Cheer
20	The Joy of Love
21	The Sun Rising Burnished
22	Fancied the Pants
23	Heart Attack
24	Close Your Eyes

SECOND SECTION

26	Our Love Enthralled
27	Empty of Your Taking
28	To Find You My Patrish
29	In All So Fair, Allow
30	A Pure Vintage
31	To Our Earth's Ends
32	So Soft Spoken
33	Into My World Surround
34	Loving So Dare
35	Little House Wren
36	My Mind's Recesses
37	Poem Amours
38	Silken Words Spoke to Us
39	The Tastes of Love
40	Strauss Waltz
41	Telling Mischief of Love

42	Courtly Love
43	This Bards Draw of Arrow
44	Such Pain in My Sorrow
45	Fresh Love New
46	All Year Through
47	Those of All Please
48	Orphic Rapture
49	Ah Love, the Scent Fresh
50	Lust like Comets
51	Whispers on the Wind
52	Racing like a Sprint Here
53	Tender My Thoughts
54	Heart of my Heart
55	My World in View
56	Feeling of Joy and Vim
57	Sweet Spots (uncensored)
58	Cast On We Drift
59	Perhaps Painless
60	Red Rose, Poem and Locket
61	Sonnets Then To Express
62	The Scent of Rose
63	Gifts Worthy of the Magi
64	I Meant to Write
65	Mistakes Too Make Progress
66	Jasmine the Sweet Perfume
67	Word Soon Spread Out

68	Movie Called Silk
69	For You There's Doubt
70	There's No Magic
71	Being of Worth Knowing
72	Come Thou Softly
73	Even In Form Gifted
74	Ill-Gotten Love
75	Come a Thither
76	I Her Thief Abet
77	My Love Outshines
78	Removes This Curse
79	Only To Weep
80	Love Sore and Languish
81	Her Dreams of Boys as Men
82	I Can Hardly Contain My Glee

THIRD SECTION

84	EOC Office
85	Then They Deny This Too
86	Nine Out of Ten
87	Were You Spying On Me
88	A Girl Bonnie, a Skirt
89	Awake I'll Try
90	I Am But Girl, Pampered
91	It's Called Dancing

92	Springs a Popping
93	The Wind to Blow
94	I Write of Spring
95	Spring Freeze
96	Think of Resort
97	Recall the Snow Falling
98	My Roses Grown in Pots
99	White Ribbons
100	So Much Out There
101	Nature's Gambles
102	A Place Special
103	Brown Eyes Saw Him
104	I've Missed All the Pursuits
105	I'm Here to Love You

FOURTH SECTION

108	This Sets the Stage
109	Drink Not the Wine of Love
110	My Wisdom Not Taken
111	Not All Is Trickery of Knave
112	Call This Nonsense
113	Flinging Kisses
114	Grievous Harm Doth Appear
115	Three Scant-O-Grace
116	Beer to All that Came

117	By Ship from Port, Forthwith
118	Along River Liffey
119	About Sprites Thick
120	Trouble She Feared
121	Pardons Given
122	While Away, Grow Old
123	Puck's Drops
124	I Have Often Dreamt
125	Such of Foolish Talk
126	Tant Pis Mortals
127	My Tears Fall Tonight
128	I Hope I Write More Soon
129	Ryback Captured
130	Makes Little Matter Who Won
131	Jack, That's Me You-all
132	Our Raid Covert

ABOUT THE AUTHOR

Acknowledgments

There are people that have helped me understand the complexities of writing good poems. Unsung heroes I honor them. They are poets who once a month come to the Black Cat Book Store in Truth or Consequences, New Mexico to both listen and recite their poems. A more jovial crowd I would be hard pressed to assemble. There is no rancor, no hoots and hollers, no getting up and storming out; these poets respect each and every one of the poems, whether they be verse, sonnets, or prose. I salute them all.

Introduction

Poems have always held in fascination to me. I find that my writing of poems, however, has begun following a heart and mind trauma, namely love affairs. This was true in high school and again in college; the last poem being written in 1959. A few of these are chronicled in various poems I have written.

I again started my writing shortly after my wife died on May 3, 2011 with my first poems having a date of July 19, 2011. This made the hiatus just over fifty years.

In most of my early poems I wrote mainly in meter and rhyme and they were about grieving, pets, love, adventure and other everyday events; it wasn't until January 5, 2012 that I had enough courage to write sonnets. Since that date I have penned over 365 sonnets and for every three poems I continue to write, two will be sonnets.

I am not an expert, more an admirer of the sonnet form. Perhaps mine fall into the format of William Shakespeare, but I really am not that concerned that they follow particular style. They are of fourteen lines, of meter and for the most part having words of two syllables or less. They are further broken into three stanzas of four lines with a couplet. The rhyming is 1-3, 2-4 and 1-2 in the couplet. I have tried to have a positive direction Iambic, but I imagine there are numerous poems that are neutral or even negative. In any case my main attention has been to myself and the reader, in other words, does the line you are reading make sense.

I dare lecture on how to read my sonnets for I expect all to be having their own way of doing so. I do offer suggestion to perhaps aid a beginning reader. Take your time reading a sonnet. There may be words that are not familiar (look up their meaning in a College level dictionary), words that are foreign and again all that I have used are in the same dictionary. Lastly, try to sing the words in the meter given. Once you get the swing of things, sonnets are fun to read. And yes, the couplet more or less ties everything together.

Now to the sonnets in this book; they are all similar in format. I have grouped them lightly and I say that because even a love sonnet might be about animals. I have also kept them in the order they were written. Some sonnets may refer to a previous sonnet and of course with the stories they are in sequence. I will not give you my reasons for writing a particular sonnet; it may have been from my growing up, my affairs amour, a movie or song heard, history or out of the blue. This latter being from what I call one-liners. I try to keep a note pad close as opening lines come to me at various moments. I write them down and then later see where they lead. Perhaps 80 percent of my poems are started with no idea of how they will read when finished. That is the wonder of writing poetry.

The first poem, "Let's Not Be Coy" is my introduction to this book of sonnets. My hope is that this sonnet will set the stage for those listed in the four sections of this book.

The first section contains 21 sonnets and begins with 17 that are about my own writing of them. The last 4 are on death.

The second section contains the most sonnets, 57 and they are about love. Love gained, love lost, love wished for, love of rue and perhaps love of love as Don Juan, but I didn't write of him. A number of sonnets are written, as much as possible, in the language of a particular period. Obviously English wasn't the language used in ancient Ireland so there are exceptions.

The third section has 22 sonnets. The first grouping is about women and is 8 in number. This is followed by 9 which I group as weather. The last 5 are animal/bird sonnets.

The fourth section of 25 sonnets starts with the first of my stories. There are 15 sonnets of the English group known by its leader as Young Sir. The next 4 are mainly fantasy sonnets that fit into this section. The last grouping of 6 is of Captain Ryback and Jack, episodes that take place in an earlier time in America, most likely the Civil War.

Some may say that writing stories in sonnet form destroys the continuity of the story. I agree and disagree. For longer stories the form of rhymed and metered verse might be better. However, with my stories each separate sonnet can be taken as a whole, while the same may not be said of an epic poem.

I have written these sonnets to chronicle my life in various stages; to assemble them as my looking glass memoirs for my children and grandchild, and dear friends.

Stanley Paul Thompson, 2012

Dedication

I dedicate this, my first book of poetry to my late wife, Patricia Anne (Trissler) Thompson. Had she not passed to our Lord, after being my soul mate for exactly fifty years, I very much doubt that I would have restarted my writing of poems.

I also dedicate these poems to my daughter, Barbara Anne Thompson and my son, Michael Paul Thompson along with his daughter, my only grandchild, Maiah DeeAnne Thompson.

There are many dear friends that have also encouraged me to write and I include them here in my dedication. They are Carroll Mae (Shaft) Springmeyer, Bruce A. Purdie and his late wife, Patricia Marguerite (Pelinka) Purdie and Maxine (Bultman) Severson. In addition, I thank my Brunch for Lunch ladies that have always been interested in what poems I had written each week.

To all, and pray I have forgotten none, I say thank you from my heart.

Sonnets

of Life Well Spent

Let's Not Be Coy

This poem, nay sir sonnet, is of form grand
Written to please and to comfort, thus said
For I to pen other this book in hand
Might then debase my poems, sully when read

But see for I've written in form august
Every word and rhyme to infuse belief
If in doldrums perhaps a poem of trust
Or of aching heart one of love relief

There are sonnets that tell tales most roguish
Of Elves, Sprites and Fairies that plan mischief
Peruse of those sacred that salve anguish
Or take sides with lovers having a tiff

Here they are my sonnets, read and enjoy
Savor those of favor, let's not be coy

First Section

Steno Tablet

Spirals go on and on, stop when wires end
When pulled vibrate to and fro like a spring
And when static hold fast paper when penned
Return button when pushed, doorbell to ring

A hole is seen, no sir, what's seen beyond
Empty of life, a hole lets out the breath
When fed, a hole swallows and then is gone
You hold a hole only when whole its width

A line appears level, when viewed up close
But bends to curve the earth, when viewed a far
A dot, a spot of ink, freckles on nose
The end of a sentence; of blood a war

This my steno tablet, simple it be
Written, becomes this poem for all to see

Lay Forth Your Poems

I know a man who you can trust your life
He'll not demand payment for acts in aid
Of stock, jovial, not brash, urbane, no wife
Sincere; man with honor, never to jade

And when dining; gentle person with class
Partakes not of spirits or smokes of dope
Wide spread knowledge, but of occult, he'll pass
Perhaps if asked sincere, he'll write of hope

He's a poet that he avers, so take warning
His minds a trap; recall nuance when said
Never writes with anger; poems not harming
But watch with care, he might just pen what fed

Salve on gallant man of sonnets written
Lay forth your poems, for all will be smitten

Little Comfort Felt in Wishful Thinking

Savoring these most pleasant moments of dawn
I've drank my brew, café noir so pleasing
Eaten my toast made of neo Tuscan
My world open, thoughts so doré teasing

I watch amazed at the Sparrow's gambit
Luring the Cat away from put-out scraps
And then quickly snatches a crumb, jam wet
The Cat seeming nonplused curls up and naps

The streets bustle, cars honk, the day begins
My friend, in love, hand-in-hand, blasé
His girl twirls, now gamine, mouth pouts, and wins
I sigh, such love I yearn starting my day

Little comfort felt in wishful thinking
I must clear my head now, get to writing

Fervent Passion

With my chores done, early morning suits me
I sit at ease, stockinged feet at beds end
Grabbing my pen and pad, ponder, should be
Sonnet my first chosen; does my heart rend

For in sorrow or angst I find the task daunting
On the other hand might joyous dawn cause
My pen to leap forward, each line vaunting
I then implore that such fervor not pause

With my music swelling, in due fashion
Such light tingling felt in my limbs, begins
What my elfin friends call fervent passion
I have then found love's cure, never at ends

Cherish then these moments of sweet repose
Let my heart bring forth love poems I compose

Washed Then Away These Hurts

You can tell my heart has been most distressed
Such is pathos, it causes lack of resolve
I long for my sonnets to be caressed
Have them savored, tasting each line of love

I feel I have failed; too late now to fix
And I am so out-and-out lost in thoughts
Baneful is my lot now, taking my licks
Truly, I need comfort, help to pass naughts

To soothe these, my aching poems so maligned
Perhaps a soak in the healing waters
I could write there steaming sonnets that rhymed
Told of love not dying, love that matters

Slowly I will surface, my life anew
Washed then away these hurts, replaced by you

Some Say He Flew Away

Some say he flew away but then God knew
Others, the no sayers, just put him gone
When asked; explain just why you think you do
None could but say, except, he went, passed on

In time as all history, it wasn't recalled
Ages went by as they are wont, some say
That is until a mere scivner enthralled
With the obscure sonnets of a past day

As he read his fervor increased greatly
Running from his cubic he cried, I know
Fellow workers stared in wonder gaily
They knew of his research, therefore his glow

Printed, now all could see; praised by heathen
Yes, a poet long past wrote of Heaven

Listen

Listen, can you hear the words now forming
As the music floats towards my ears hearing
I write their beat, my pen again storming
Rapid my thoughts; suffer some worth bearing

Wonder if in silence I could write poems
Do I require those sounds, must I admit
Only I will ever know where truth blooms
But the songs or artists aid I submit

Forgo the croons of love ballads; not I
Perhaps the mood pulse my fingers just so
Extracts the phrase, rhyme and meter I lay
A Pound Will might offer to guess my know

Tell me as you have read what songs were played
Or the artist's name or type of tune laid

Escape in Thought

When I look out I see the world around
I can't vision the world, those times before
My birth sets forth the start I see surround
And my death will mark the end; views no more

I thought about this, I even pondered
Wondered what my father saw then prior
Were there sunsets that awed him, sights garnered
Did he think what a son might see after

Reckon he did not as only poets
 Spend their time thus thinking about these things
Who else will man the walls circled by moats
Fending off the arrows, writing of kings

Do not judge me if I escape in thought
Just join in and savor my poems here brought

The Task So Hard

Emma is Jane Austen's maker of matches
Solving the heart's delights of friends she knows
I do suspect she was afraid; love hatches
To be caught up wanting marriage, her vows

A strong novel of pure romance given
Much like Shakespeare's plays, the missteps building
But then that is true art, not pulp riven
Master story tellers, their works gilding

I too feel their ardor, play the amour
What could be more fine than loving fully
Well there's writing sonnets; love by poems lore
For I to choose betwixt is such folly

The task so hard, fourteen lines I'm rationed
Against Austen's Emma thousands mentioned

My Three Poems Tonight

I must abhor doldrums for they besmirch
Try to remain blithesome through thick and thin
And I must be doing well in skirmish
It is battle; being steadfast within

My time to write is at nightfall's quiet
With my music, mostly it is background
I find easy the words put no riot
Thoughts go thither, so I follow the sound

Past now midnight I feel content, awake
May then at dawn rue my reckless manner
For sleep is prime, it fuels whatever I take
So soon I'll close my pad and rest garner

I have gotten then my three poems tonight
Happy at last I will slumber, not write

Sometimes I Feel Mauldin

Sometimes I feel maudlin and not from drink
Times when my poems wax in bathos forethought
I shan't complain for my sonnets might wink
At love sordid, but not romance when sought

Tonight I am trying, but that's excuse
The mood changing; my mind wanders about
Perhaps the hour, lateness portends recluse
I'm quite happy, enjoy these hours throughout

Surprised that I've written sonnets as well
At first they scared, meter and rhyme set forth
But then practice, violà tout rings the bell
Now I hardly write poems other of worth

Sometimes I feel cheerful, even elated
Writing sonnets witty never abated

That's a Job for Goblins

Like a blizzard I'm hit with pains quite small
But they add up burying your soul en fin
Once I could dig, clear a pathway, save all
Now the job is harder, takes more time off

Don't get concerned, I still can do the work
It just takes me longer, got to pace things
People like me survive, detours we fork
A path of no great harm, just our goings

Sometimes I might wonder, is it a game
Like we are all in a big bowl, confined
With these players looking in, their ballgame
If so then I must be a star, defined

Trying to sum up all human problems
In a sonnet, that's a job for Goblins

Let Me Dream This Tonight

Quickly I write before candle's light out
So much to say, dare I've time now I pray
Might then the moon give me light enough without
My poor fingers are near frozen this way

Scribble this nub pencil, barely I see
Was that love or lave I wrote so dainty
Little the change be as love I leave thee
So poor the mice left my empty pantry

I should give up as a poet's life's hard
So few I've sold, even for loaf of bread
I need my poems printed, not penned on card
One said that my sonnets barely be read

Let me dream this tonight, might a patron
Feeling sorry offer to take me on

Will of the Gods

What if this had to go before this write
That my sonnets were picked, ready to book
I have enough now written, I can pick right
So this becomes surplus, I'm off the hook

Except I wasn't to know; kept in the dark
The book's message would change someone's resolve
What, I have not figured out yet the mark
But of moment it is, I have to solve

This will take some doing, going through poems
I don't even know what poem to look for
Maybe it is more than one; are there bombs
Is it a code to solve, should help be more

I haven't answered the big question; what odds
Is this out of my hands, will of the gods

Time Wasted in Rhyme

It feels like my life is being sped up
Certain events which I do in order
Like lunch, a nap, dinner, they all pickup
Happen like they were just moments prior

I then wonder is this normal aging
Because I can recall when young the wait
When just the next weekend seemed long staging
And you could spend lifetimes asking for date

So then I'm not surprised that time flows by
I can sit here quiet, no urge to ire
Or write myself a poem or two to bye
The night away then close my eyes, retire

Perhaps this is just time wasted in rhyme
That all is now perceived as sped up time

Welcome the Cheer

Give your speaking of a barkeep rousing
Throw it out, let timbers quake in rafters
My play performs in an open housing
Where hoots and such often upstage actors

If you are good-tempered, can stand insults
And dodge thrown fruit you may find good applause
And then all the strain gives warm felt results
And as actors you'll be feted because

But should the boos concern and cause alarm
The crowd will be austere in their conduct
And if ireful become provoked to harm
I've known tar and feather the price mistook

Some here recall I give this talk sincere
Our play enjoyed by all, welcome the cheer

The Joy of Love

Tell it from your heart, let joy spill outward
That's what the man had said, need he try now
For as deep as he could recall no word
Or phrase or even sentence lie there he'd vow

For the best part of a week, could be two
He racked his brain trying hard to figure
What was within his heart, was the item new
Something he had lately felt of nurture

Then as things oft happen, out of the blue
He knew what the man had spoken there of
It was his gift to pen sonnets of woo
For those poems spoke fervid the joy of love

And in a flash do lines of rhyme appear
As the poet structure meter sincere

The Sun Rising Burnished

They have given pencil and some paper
Said I could write a note, have it sent too
I think at dawn it will come down; death sir
At least they are civil; wish them thorough

Just think of me being away for long
That I may once return, don't hold out hope
I shall be there waiting, welcome thereon
Life will pass so quickly, hold on and cope

I have starred at death and seen his black eyes
He does not scare me, one sent not from God
I shall feel no pain in death, the beast lies
There is no hell, only that which we've trod

I hear them now coming, this note finished
Dawn breaks early, the sun rising burnished

Fancied the Pants

I'm just middling, perhaps second-rate bore
Barely had I made it out of my high school
College was not for me, thought I'd try Corps
Fancied the pants, stripping, that was so cool

Stuck me on the first wave at Iwo Jima
Puny Island, Japs said to be dug in
We'd have to get drawings of their schema
Landing boats all around, rough sea, can't swim

Ramp just lowered, we have to wade ashore
Getting wet to my crotch, sand in my boots
Looks like we are in free, a walk-on tour
Rest up me lads, I hope climbing hills suits

Most of us have dropped our gear, it's too hot
There's a cave, I wonder was that a sh...

Heart Attack

Shivers, I've had them bad every day since
It's not a cold, it's not the flu; neither
I hear my name; take your picture, I wince
Then they start, slow at first, won't stop either

And my heartbeats rapid; I feel its surge
Am I having attack, should I rest more
The sound deafens, my head plays the drum dirge
Now in panic; someone...medic...call for

The sweats begin, I feel clammy, less sure
All sounds now are muted, vision is blurred
I feel their hands, my arm feels the pressure
I'm now moving, I see myself, not heard

Then in silence, the whole collage; I'm wheeled
Film stop action, voices mime words revealed

Close Your Eyes

It's dark in here; what's that you say to me
Close your eyes, then let your mind see wonder
Oh now I see; this is Heaven surely
But the brightness prevents what's seen yonder

You must forget sounds, sights, human events
There's no body, no pain, only of thought
And the wonder; nothing before invents
But see here, I've spoken; no more, it's naught

No more words said, ever, then how address
My mind, well I suppose I had one now
Then I knew the answer, thinking redress
Pretty cool I thought, then response felt, wow

For all of you humans there's no insight
Only death will bring the wonder I cite

Second Section

Our Love Enthralled

I tried last night to sleep but sleep was naught
Soft sounds were made to haste my rest, alas
My mind engrossed in thoughts, rampant there brought
Of you, my fair, our love I do repass

I'll write a note this day, this hour to you
Pen words so sweet their scents attract lone bees
In form of poem my heart entreats so true
Feelings, deep down, I pour my love in ease

Addressed to you, I'll spur the mail so sent
That on morrow the note you'll get, held fast
To read, to feel the pulse of me so lent
Then to clasp fast to breast, entwined at last

And then come night I'll sleep of dreams recalled
To wake at day, refreshed, our love enthralled

Empty of Your Taking

When I'm in this dreamy sort of temper
And the music is sweet, I'll think of you
For songs of love remind of times after
When we spoke in murmurs so no one knew

Lying in bed, I place you here beside
You'll touch, only finger tips, to my lips
I'll kiss them one by one, passions, abide
Then my lips to brush, so lightly on trips

In mind I find these things imagined, sensual
My thoughts drifting, slowly, enter slumber
And if dreaming, perchance I then recall
Your warmth and scent so au fait in ember

And then as I awake, the dawn breaking
My bed, much tossed, empty of your taking

To Find You My Patrish

I pour out my heart to you my flowers
Let this life blood add the nourish which so
Brings out nectar, so sweet, that it powers
My poor struggling ardent passion to grow

Then in Diana's forest let me then rest
And pray bring forth Fairies to soothe my soul
For on morrow, quickened, harness my quest
To find you my Patrish, my love, my goal

Dormant now, I dream in lustrous colors
Of green bowers of grapes and red berries
And there waiting, my loved princess, dolors
Then she sees me enter, our greet marries

So much love I imbue, accept withal
Of my guileless promise to keep eternal

In All So Fair, Allow

I've stared many a night with sight unseen
Just gazing, trying hard to focus
As thoughts of you, swirling around, seem lean
I lack the means, needing hocus-pocus

You went away I guess, to think of me
Am I just a problem needing deep thought
Really, it's not complex at all; easy
I won't demand of you replete love brought

Just a moment is all I need, and yet
I'd take as much as you would let me have
Always hoping; mindful, tempus fugit
But come what may, happy I'd be with lave

Oh my sweet dear, just a glimpse I seek now
To see you there, in all so fair, allow

A Pure Vintage

I'm a vessel needing something to hold
Useless standing still here in need of fill
Will you help me; pour some nectar when told
With its sweetness attract someone at will

I can hold much talent, some of genius
And if some spills, matter not in toto
I can pour love filling throughout venous
Empty, thirsting, those want of yours so-so

Then sit me still, sealed, so I'll not spoil
And when of need draw some from the bottle
Use when tumult occurs or when you toil
And should of love require, use of pottle

For years I might rest here, a pure vintage
Until one day someone's need have assuage

To Our Earth's Ends

I can't be sure why I love you, honest
All my feelings are on auto pilot
Perhaps a gem moonstone struck me, fondest
For its Opal essence obscures a lot

I can't wander here forever my sweet
With daze, I see wonder, such grand passion
And pray to hold your heart and kiss your feet
Greater would I swoon in raptures mansion

There to hold you tightly, least you vanish
Being taken from me, I'd lie in pain
Then with heroes effort, wield sword, banish
All who'd do this ghastly scatheful, most bane

Oh my darling, my most precious flower
To our Earth's ends would I travel, I aver

So Soft Spoken

I dreamt of you in lush bowers so sought
Your hair adorned with pink Primrose, woven
In plaits hanging and with Forget-me not
And white Love-on-a-mist, in rows all even

Pedals of Rose lay at your feet, cushioned
No sound is made walking along arbor
In sight I see Fairies, lilting, intoned
Flutters of wings, fussing, of loves labor

Were you aware of me, I think it not
Your eyes appeared not to focus ahead
My voice, silent, called out, then cried for naught
When I awoke, damp marks of tears my bed

These dreams, they sap puissance, I tire often
Draining my voiced resolve, so soft spoken

Into My World Surround

There is sweetness I taste thinking of you
Sometimes it is lemon without tang's tick
Other times its berry flavor quite new
Never have I tasted the sour acerbic

Alone I sense aroma of the bouquet
That you bring now into my world surround
Essences of rare perfumes that sate and stay
Valiant, I now seek out those Sprites abound

And come slumber I dream of you fondly
My mind cautious of what my heart palpates
Dreamy I write romance rondelles soundly
And then proudly proclaim as my estates

Come the morning I hear pitter-patter
My mind waking, it's not you I gather

Loving So Dare

I thought about your note regarding Friday
Having to then cancel because of moil
It's not doomsday, just a schedule delay
And if Monday suits us, we'll chat awhile

It's hard, perhaps for me, as I'm retired
And not working, but you very much depend
On your on-call service, even if tired
Forgive my haste, I wish not to append

Let me write then in poem for I'm bemused
Thinking of you, even rapture falls short
For in sonnet all love pours forth enthused
Seeking elfin abettors as my cohort

Be thus aware that this poet fights fair
In his approach towards loving so dare

Little House Wren

Little House Wren hopping along outside
With your tail high, seeking what food you could
Are you bothered that I watch from inside
I'd hide if you complain, really I would

Patterned brown shades, you strike handsome poses
Flitting now to yard plants, insects beware
His sharp dagger like bill spears in Roses
Then in a flash you're gone, startled, I stare

Out of my sight I hear your song rattling
Are you calling a mate with such loudness
For she answers, then much hubble-bubbling
Another male Wren the cause, fussy business

I thought of you later at sun setting
I was the Wren singing, my heart letting

My Mind's Recesses

My thoughts, they are for you, persona grata
Safely stored here, away from those seeking
You have the key, take one or et cetera
Enjoy in the rapture I hold keeping

My dreams unlocked, there where you can always
Explore my mind's recesses, hidden from view
There you'll find places I've picked and kept, byways
Seldom traveled where love heightens anew

My hopes are shared; such of wonder they are
Happy blithe in life's most mundane event
No fears approach and no dangers lay bare
We live in peace and share blissful fervent

Oh my darling, my sweet, such love I bring
Joined as one we drink eternal life's spring

Poem Amours

You have given me a reason to write
Of love, of my yearning to now express
Deep thoughts hidden neath my bastion, contrite
I am grateful and yet rue my trespass

For I have used you most unfair in love
I once said to perpend me mad in deed
Carried away in my fervent quest of
Loving when I knew I would not succeed

And now you have gently reproved advance
Yet left open meetings in time apart
I rush to say accept, and if perchance
A show or a concert we might take part

My life evolves with friendship liken ours
Let me then pledge not love, but poem amours

Silken Words Spoke to Us

I write out my sonnets like threads of silk
Each one caressed; wanting to hold them dear
Approved, each line writes as mother's rich milk
Giving nurture and strength offered sincere

Of love, the silk woven with no rending
But tight and strong, innate fabric now said
With thought, web like weave lets discern accessing
For poems spoken test of freedoms most staid

Born from cocoons, fables fondly enchant
Of Sprites, Fairies, hoyden Elf's; their blithe romps
Should then per chanced arranged, a rogue encamped
His mad gambols receive their taunts and bumps

My heart yells out in joy when I pen thus
Such love I score, silken words spoke to us

The Tastes of Love

At times my heart spill'th of love about
From boughs sweetened flowers I lay entranced
Willing the scents; perfumed to float throughout
Where they waff in wondrous pleasures romanced

Wouldst thou enter, pulled in by sweet bouquets
Join with me in rapture, my wish answered
Oh my cosset comes where we'll be gourmets
Sampling the tastes of love, our time treasured

Later whilst our passion mellows slowly
We bask in late suns warmth holding close by
Then in spoon-like embrace repose lowly
Sleeping deep whilst blissful dreams soothe and sigh

Awakened, the dew wetting now my ardor
But the dream still lingered, wishing you more

Strauss Waltz

Oh the waltz, such beauty, beating rhythm
Johann Strauss, the Second, king of the best
I know not of whether to march to them
Or clap my hands, bow, whirl, dance, or just rest

Listening, I dare you to sit still; see there
Your feet keeping the one-two-three beating
And do I now detect your head sway near
Imagine the pomp, gaiety, skirts all billowing

And then that stiff soldier stomping downbeat
And you're away, cape thrown, medals jangling
With your partner smiling, you both twirl neat
All eyes upon you now, forelock dangling

The waltz, certain to raise spirits soaring
The Strauss music, ever to be roaring

Telling Mischief of Love

With poems I write telling mischief of love
For bards narrate the changing events of life
And not all of amour, that be sure of
For in darken spaces lurks there the knife

Those that dwell on pain most severe take heed
No just profit you will obtain with spite
Hearts sores languish in thoughts; revenge I need
Will not appease, rather come back to bite

Learn you, not of mordant thoughts and wishing
Savor what you recall of most pleasant
Be not mindful of what's bathos pressing
Soon it not be gotten memory recent

Stories of loves travails pens the poet
Who else love's God Venus let be known's it

Courtly Love

Of times ago; I dream to be there now
Is it wistful longing, am I homesick
The past draws me nearer, to whom I bow
For she waits most resigned, the queen I pick

Approached I see her face, beckons come near
Emotive feelings fill me, dare a tear fall
She in beauty, I claim no looks of peer
Yet there is sign; welcome to the Queen's Ball

I must be tongue-tied, I stammer; may I
A smile, oh most splendrous rapture complete
I bow, then she curtsies, our dance we vie
Around we whirl, dancing until deplete

We have complied, acts of courtly love known
Slowly I back away, fading what shown

This Bards Draw of Arrow

I would wish it so, to give love a chance
To bid me, come welcome to join at last
Alas, all that I do is dream romance
That I endure; my life paltry at best

In what I write; sonnets so pure foretells
Those in splendid rapture of loves delight
But wish I might, no love befalls or dwells
In my empty heart, nor any in sight

Perhaps I shall rest here easy, reposed
And let Cupid's bow fling arrows at will
For then surely one will strike fair exposed
And then she will thither come by my spell

For such is life; this bards draw of arrow
Who pens love for all, lives on in sorrow

Such Pain in My Sorrow

There was a time, not long ago recalled
When breath of warm perfumed air came floating
To sun drenched spots where lay my soul enthralled
Such of heady rapture I felt gloating

And now I weep for loss suffered; contrite
What breeze wafts is biting, cold and scentless
I see flowers stunted for lack of light
And clouds cover where I now lie senseless

Such pain in my sorrow, must it persist
My heart's sluggish from the wrenching taken
I know my life's ending, as fate will insist
That such dourness never will love waken

But cry; bring anew sunlight with blown fragrance
Infuse my whole, save this poor love's romance

Fresh Love New

I've been remiss my sweet for poems of love
Those most joyful moments come now to share
All else is past, for now hold hearts above
I thus shower you with flowers most faire

I'll dream this night only of you with me
Pleasant the scenes, of springs freshened woodlands
Wherein birds court in their brilliant finery
And Fox kits make squinting eyes for suntans

Of such idyllic dreams to enthrall slumber
I wish this dream to go for times ever
But soon morning awakens, my love fonder
My thoughts now but images, fading never

This my sonnet of love I send to you
May it cheer your heart this day, fresh love new

All Year Through

Often I pause during the day and think
What is making this day special to me
Is it breathing fresh air, eating and drink
Have I received a note or a package marked free

Maybe it is nothing like those mentioned above
Would it be, nah it couldn't; but then maybe
Because I'm in dreamland, floating on love
Wouldn't that be a kick in the pants; yesiree

This state is so pleasing I might yell out
I'm in love, I'm in love; people hear this
And then follow with such dancing about
Add some rain; Gene Kelly, I'd be in bliss

What a wonder is my romance of you
That I'd do this every day, all year through

Those of All Please

Bring me of speech, I ask that it be plain
For my heart is empty; it pains when beats
And none would cure this break of heart so lain
But come ye of love, then the past retreats

Bring me a gift, I ask that be paltry
For to assuage my now doleful bad spell
No brought present would cheer, all is tawdry
Yet send a rose, so sweet it cures me well

Bring me your hand, I see you wear no band
Then our wedded union now is broken
And if you wish that I perpend; remand
Reflect, then wear your ring, true love spoken

All that I ask, simple treasures are these
Love, a rose and marriage; those of all please

Orphic Rapture

Where have you gone muse of mine for ever
Have I wandered the fens alone in spring
Are you not pleased with my sonnets clever
Did I slight you in ways of my offering

Let me beguile in poems goddess so faire
By words entreat blessed favor of me
Let me lay of sounds true, orphic rapture
To lull of sleep, wondrous feelings to be

Then when awake, restore thy muse I plead
For then humbly I'll pen sonnets praising
With much delight lyrics extol engraved
Thus all will see gracious of our blessing

All my heart and soul I pledge my dear muse
Those poems of love, despair, and hope enthuse

Ah Love, the Scent Fresh

Ah love, the scent fresh, now enters young men
Their eyes seeking; wanton with brash visions
Spied now fair lasses; contrive larkish strat'gem
Making complete fools in this their missions

But love, never-the-less endures heedless
Some of lasting romance, others of rue
And shy maidens; those not wanting recess
Prolong the game of love; their flirty imbues

Often there is observed bluster amongst males
Liken to their mimic cockfight contests
Rarely to blows, but quite heated entails
Their plucky ardor compels, rightly insists

This the springtime that stirs fervent passions
For young lovers sense this change in fashions

Lust like Comets

Does a poet spin tales telling of him
Are these written poems then yearnings for love
Unmasked the truth be told, his goals are dim
But he will march forward, blindly much of

Let us suppose that this is true; so what
Are not all men able, at least ardent
Showing great of tender feelings so sought
But young girls prefer lust, shun men who couldn't

So I offer these of common knowledge
Penning sonnets of love is most condign
Just don't get caught acting out the poems pledge
Accept this role, making young hearts gladden

I'll ask once more, do poets live their sonnets
Spoken to me in hush, lust like comets

Whispers on the Wind

Whispers on the wind I recall from you
Soft hushes and mews caress and soothe my ear
Ever telling me of your love so true
Whispers, how I wish I might hear them here

Drifting off now, daydreams become my meets
I then select the one I've stored away
Our first meeting, the warmth I felt at greets
Such of wonder your voice, the trill and sway

A knock, I know what's next, why won't they stay
My dream now not wanting to let me go
There now, are you awake; good, take these pray
I will mouth them, later spit them out though

Now I'm alone again, I search for wind
She's left window open; whispers you send

Racing like a Sprint Here

We spoke, our hearts sensing each the other
Now there was no pausing, comfort it felt
Telling of those mundane facts than rather
Broach of love now gnawing like a tight belt

You would tell me, loosen it then withal
And I would with mildly averse agree
But still deep down feelings greater enthrall
Accept I must these rules, let love still be

I have told you before that I'm ardent
For not being poet I would then aver
Thus it is my nature, none less is lent
Like a puppy I live for love ever

Cool then my heart, racing like a sprint here
Let the morrow bring a calmness manner

Tender My Thoughts

Tender my thoughts of you I send tonight
For you shall hear them as they leave most kind
Einstein said they travel at speed of light
And who am I that would refute that mind

Of such splendor I craft, made thus in poem
Nay, not just a poem, but sonnet in form
Those of mortal fame doth guide all that's known
And some of not, bespoke, thus be quorum

Of the sonnet I speak the most fondly
A verse of such beauty used in meter
To write one is gifted in thought soundly
And when spoken in truth is grand theater

Let them fly then at speed unheard to you
To be read as my pen writes words so true

Heart of my Heart

Heart of my heart, beating only for me
Such of tender pulses they massage softly
Quicken my thoughts of love I have for thee
I rush towards the dawn with my head held lofty

I will then give myself for you to take
With ring to bear witness my pledge of wed
Oh joy complete, let this day then partake
Our banns to be published, that it be said

Let doubts be rent, only good thoughts persist
I have means; we'll not be wanting of pay
A home awaits us, a wee cottage I list
Or a hearthstone of name, quite large they say

Then too, there is for both of us to bear
Lord John and my Lady Sarah, such pair

My World in View

Starlight, moonlight is all one needs to see
For night is my realm of life, my cosmic
In its stillness, in its mystique I'll be
There to enthrall, there to enchant so quick

If you will then explore throughout the night
Out of earshot, out of eyesight, alone
In the crannies, the cragged shadows of light
There pause silent, let your senses now then hone

Then close your eyes, visions I'll let converge
Wondrous beauties of the night soon abound
Sparkles brighter than of diamonds emerge
Raptures you have never known all surround

This you may have; fulfill your life anew
Should you choose to enter my world in view

Feeling of Joy and Vim

Sonnets of love I've brought straight from my heart
Lines of wondrous rhyme and meter flowing
To you enchant with such passion impart
That when couplet's read your face is glowing

As the stanzas build my fervid mind soars
Telling of loves pleasures in hushed whispers
Listen, hear my heart beats, their sound now roars
Calm me quickly with kisses, assuage despairs

Laying in the stillness our hearts entwined
My pulse now slowed, moments we will recall
Fondness becomes of us, romance combined
We are content, cares have vanished withal

To rise at dawn feeling of joy and vim
Hoping he'll send sonnets of love again

Sweet Spots (uncensored)

Do we all have a sweet spot worth knowing
Like a home run swing that hits the ball neat
Or a tennis ball smacked center mass string
Then there's that...I'll temper now this poems heat

Am I then a censor of my thoughts here
Are we not all mature, those that read poems
So that sweet spot no doubt is known my dear
With some practice one can hit home run moans

But I detour on my question first asked
I can think of one, the palm of my hand
The soft fleshy part in center when tasked
There a ball caught might hurt, but stays whence land

You might take pause and think of your sweet spot
I'm sure there are many spots you have got

Cast On We Drift

I write tonight of a sonnet so pure
The sounds of Chris Botti's trumpet guides me
Subtle the soft horn blows, my poem now sure
Meant to entice your love asked for freely

Let your dreams flow as the river's portent
No dam to hold and still, it runs free of
I'll ride atop my craft being natant
Listening to the ripples telling of love

Then in a back water, caught we'll rest there
And hear the leaves rustle the wind causing
Till a nudge makes us move, once more we wear
Then with relief finds our body pausing

We've come to the ending, slow our motion
Cast on we drift now part of the ocean

Perhaps Painless

I didn't want you to leave me, not that way
Suppose I made the wrong move, I ask why
And you gave me clues, what was I to say
That I love you, wouldn't that have been a lie

Must I now do penance; just tell me how
I'll bleed sorrow; let flow freely, replete
I could tear out my heart; would you allow
For the damage might wound my pride complete

Each night I'll stand below your dorm window
If rain or in moonlight, keeping watch there
Show me a sign; white flag, and I'll then go
If not then eves coldness becomes the air

That I truly love thee I now confess
Should I have said before, perhaps painless

Red Rose, Poem and Locket

I gave her a red Rose, my love thus troth
Red of the blood I would gladly shed then
For if fortune fails me and war comes forth
Then in battle carry her flag again

I gave her a locket, my face therein
To wear near skin so soft, there warmth impart
Asked her to pray each night that I'm safe then
And kiss my face's image held close her heart

I gave her a love poem, twas a sonnet
In it I wrote of my love borne to her
Then at nightfall and at dawning read it
Keep firm resolve that my voice once more hear

Let the red Rose, poem and locket remind
That my love will return each night to bind

Sonnets Then To Express

Like a river running, she's called Psyche
Pursued by love's Cupid; antics my mind
His sharp arrows, love tangs, pin pricks they'll be
The dam burst, then flushed out both wet I find

Resting I shan't recall why this happened
I am benign to thoughts that have passage
Allow therein Goddess and God opened
But I firmly stand pat, there be no rage

For just last week two were lovey-dovey
Thor of war and Irene of peace, the duo
I braced for naught, their words spoken of me
Such his kindness letting our thoughts thus go

I let it be knownst that I'll take issues
Sonnets then to express written these views

The Scent of Rose

On heart strings held I strum my love to you
Pray then bear my vocals of sounds melic
For these of Greek lyric poems sung most true
I now promise, nay, pledge my life as relic

Lean forth, give thus a sign, wonder am I
Oh do not tease; my hearts beating so fast
Tis your love I seek now; steadfast I vie
Let none come here before me in contest

Is that a tear, oh pray, I'll not offend
My dunce; it's my life you worry will part
That I might die, be so folly, my end
I meant not in battle, rest still your heart

The scent of Rose I now inhale so clear
It's you my love, came here, embraced sincere

Gifts Worthy of the Magi

These gifts I lay upon your heart with care
I've thought them through, expense is no issue
For I'd borrow on time, be made aware
The cost, surely one couldn't fault this pursue

Gifts one and two are first, steadfast I pledge
This to follow with all support mustered
For these will keep me close when you're on edge
My life I then commit, rest then assured

The last number three done without status
It is simply; yes, and costly for me
But I give it freely; affects then us
The gift is love, now and ever to be

Steadfast, support and love, these my triad
The gifts worthy of the magi once said

I Meant to Write

On the grass we all lounged, evening coming
Her name was Pat, but I only saw Anne
Did she know of, even suspect roaming
I think not as we got along quite grand

That I used her I make little of fact
I was wounded, my own fault too, sanctioned
Was it rebound, perhaps; certain no tact
But we dated, our own manqué notioned

Had we romanced sooner, then fate estop
I to Navy duty, she of flight skilled
Then a few months pass by, our lives nonstop
News, her brother, Navy Pilot is killed

I meant to write, assuage her hurt, console
But her flight crashed, all dead over North Pole

Mistakes Too Make Progress

My sad sonnet; "I Meant to Write", is true
But I shan't dwell; forget, 'tis best to heal
Her death was not my fault; must I still rue
I'll try not to think, but those times were real

I've loved many; not all ended sadly
What cause, tell me, have I imperiled thusly
Were not past trysts mutual, seen not badly
That we learn from gambles, pleasant mostly

There were some false starters, not all pristine
I'm not for all gallant, some were not amused
That I did try, a few forsook my line
Maybe with more time I'd have then bemused

Through life one learns; mistakes too make progress
Accept them thus with aplomb, with no redress

Jasmine the Sweet Perfume

Where the Willows sway and ripples run on
You will find me anxious there my waiting
Come thou quickly for time will soon be gone
For at morning I'll leave to fight the King

There your scent comes, Jasmine the sweet perfume
And you framed in moonlight my heart stutters
To ask you to wait, oh dare I assume
For you are young and war's black death utters

Holding you our whispers softly saying
Tender nothings yet at moment so much
Hush now she says, her hands guide mine laying
The heat of land or is it ours as such

These were dark years, times when good men perished
And yet new born numbers increased; cherished

Word Soon Spread Out

Oh my grand sir allow me this retort
You came to me drunken and foul last night
And I smelled that perfume not mine of sort
You then passed out thus spent the night sans fight

Princess I do beseech you hear me out
All is true but not of lust most carnal
'Twas the barkeep, that plump one I've no doubt
She gave hugs and kisses at every bar call

You oaf I'll not accept this weak reply
That scent I know, 'twas than buxom barmaid
I've heard stories told of which can imply
Your tale a fib, so bed in spare room laid

Word soon spread out, the Prince now forced aside
And wives gave broad hints of sanctions far wide

Movie Called Silk

Rather think you knew, you being sublime
Were you so sure; maybe I thought so too
For in the end I did return each time
A price you paid, was the cost worth beaucoup

Perhaps we dwell too much on love flawless
Never minding what God gave to Moses
Does it really exact sin more or less
To what degree are we punished for this

I look at it this way, did it matter
We had no time-outs, no wishing it through
Our life happy, at least appeared latter
And I know in my heart our love was true

I saw tonight a good movie called Silk
It too portrayed couple much of like ilk

For You There's Doubt

Was there magic; there must have been something
For these things don't happen alone, they're planned
So the sequent question bears then listening
Who made it then befall, did fate command

Of course all of this was not on my mind
Barely twenty abstruse thoughts wouldn't occur
I just took in this good fortune in kind
Like it was my doing; held no rancor

Then why didn't it succeed; it was ample
But I'm missing the point, something to know
Surely it was bêtise, plain and simple
There wasn't magic, the end came as a blow

You may wonder what this sonnet's about
That I know is condign, for you there's doubt

There's No Magic

Perhaps I've been unfair, leaving you doubt
Let me recall this tale; could be sordid
Oh there's love, but you may have sensed that rout
Way too much to handle, I couldn't hoard it

There was pleasure and that was the quagmire
This is hard to explain, opens up thoughts
That I loved her, that much is true; no ire
My mind battered, I could lose all, these naughts

I was afraid of love complete with her
That with her a marriage would void contract
For the Navy paid my way as bursar
So purged my lust, someone else then attract

That this became known to her I take blame
There's no magic, I just couldn't play her game

Being of Worth Knowing

Can one tell of love by saying what's not
That to leave and not say goodbye is one
Or to kill or malign, surely that's naught
Or to stay in sang-froid or phlegm as done

I could go on and on listing the cons
And you would tire urging me please estop
Enough of nonsense as I might go on for eons
Then I must tell of love, making it pop

The love I view is one I espouse
If I make you happy then I am pleased
To feed, clothe, and shelter, to be my spouse
And to listen, accept your point as eased

For I see love as a river flowing
Gaining volume, being of worth knowing

Come Thou Softly

Come thou softly as I in sleep await
Enchant my heart for on morrow I seek
Your love lasting, the thrill, my fill to sate
And drink in your beauty for that I speak

It is dawn now, where art thou my servant
Fetch me trappings befit this day of cheer
For I meet my love, my learned savant
We lunch at Kings Crossing, fresh Quail and beer

There you are my flower, permit me to sit
My mind bubbles with thoughts of great degree
Allow then my betroth, as Prince my writ
To then rejoice and pray your words agree

Bravo your read, stellar job you have done
The play now to open, expect long run

Even In Form Gifted

Oh my pet I languish without your love
I will wither away, become a shell
Cast down by the waves and ground dull there of
No more of pearl luster, worthless as well

Pray show me a sign, rise up my ardor
Then be of my romance; cupid aid me
Fling straight and true arrows, give no quarter
Thence stung let loves potion impinge in thee

Send forth your handmaiden, my shell gather
Then pour on oil, color will then show through
Thus I'm transformed mother-of-pearl nacre
To sit upon your shelf a prize won true

Oh my pet my spirit is much lifted
To be with you even in form gifted

Ill-Gotten Love

Are those of ill-gotten love now clement
Wouldst they forgive this most ardent suitor
Should he beg for one more chance, a moment
To prove his worth, now in tatters, before

For them some hurts and slights are best forgot
These wounds now healed never to be opened
Then too I would agree that these be fought
Why bring up past failures, why they opined

But this is their words; have I not a voice heard
To make amends here, plead then my love again
For if romance has true merit not feared
Then by all rights I say press on most sane

Because of deep feelings in these issues
I haven't mentioned these ill-gotten miscues

Come a Thither

Whence doth my love come a thither from now
Through the far hills covered with grasses most pure
White shoes damp with smells of Thyme and Yarrow
Her face now flushed such her hurried allure

Ah, her smile bears welcome, her arms reaching
Out to me, we embrace my lips finding
Hers too and now touching, so cool each bring
Flavors of the berries she has hiding

Then arm in arm we stroll towards the town square
Mine a gentle walk, hers sashay in tease
For she is still youthful, a trait most faire
But I glance a caution, be still now please

As we enter all eyes are on my love
Her dress of blue cotton and white of glove

I Her Thief Abet

I then persisted that she act more demure
For our intent was not to gain notice
That I blame thy servant, I will assure
My own fondness, nay my rapture the price

We thus entered the pub called The Scotsman
And took a small table, darkness there found
I then made my approach to the bar man
And on key my lovely swooned and fell down

This caused turmoil, indeed for they all raced
To her aid while quietly I robbed the till
Not then observed I rushed to her most haste
Lifted her and said in child, my love's ill

We then made short our stay this faire hamlet
She a bonnie lass and I her thief abet

My Love Outshines

Such is your charm as it sparkles the air
Splendrous fireworks, oh how wondrous and fain
But have me to think; no, let's not compare
My love outshines the sun and quenches the rain

Your voice is most lyric rapture to me
I'm lulled by the music, comes it from form
You need not then import, this tune isn't free
My love out sings the wind and hushes the storm

Your waltz dances flowing of twirls most splendid
And veil bouffant blown, my eyes they did glance
Still I longed for common, jovial then rid
My love performs well of song and the dance

Cherish your love through the hills and the vales
My love there romanced with moon and Wolf wails

Removes This Curse

Soft sounds ease my troubled thoughts left crying
As if the soothe of her singing would catch falling
My loves last kisses now mere smudges drying
On lips that no longer tremble calling

I shant burden others, this pain I bear
It is my own doing, I can't erase
Nor take back the words there uttered unfair
They shall lie there and give my heart debase

Could that I might with my soul now given
Approach her faire, contrite with my penance
To once again be of favor, quicken
Thence my oath to give, revive romance

Why should I lay in bed having remorse
When just one word from her removes this curse

Only To Weep

Music, it flows nigh to caress my soul
How I wish that it too visits my love
For she bides far away being of dole
Her father, the king has been murdered there of

I will comfort her soon as plans now laid
To storm the keep, dispatch those who remain
His force can no longer defeat our raid
And thus will soon announce myself to reign

Then on that day battle did take skirmish
My own loyal fighter's victors by noon
Conquest of the castle, we'd not besmirch
Those peoples within, we came to save, not wound

Then fast I made to the king's own quarters
Only to weep for she and maid martyrs

Love Sore and Languish

Even though I weep no tears have I made
Such is my state, poignant my loss of her
I must compose, return, my love forsake
Forebear my pain, as king claim my scepter

You Grace I wish to have late king's daughter
Entombed beneath, her death declared holy
As she was killed by one loyal warrior
Not by her own hand as first told wrongly

Her tomb inscribe thus 'hic jacet Lisbeth'
And to mark this tragic event, a day
Will be a faire, ovation of life and death
This I command of you, go forth then pray

Even with a conquest there comes anguish
For the victors find love sore and languish

Her Dreams of Boys as Men

I dream of him every waking moment
He is virile and most handsome of sight
Burly and coarse, of me protect, foment
Still he's polite, pulls the chair, knows what's right

Then his loving I could not ask for more
His hair is long and soft with curls on nape
And his hands with fingers long do explore
Yet with tender whispers my thoughts escape

Oh I dream with ardent wishes he brought thus
To lay upon my bed to hold till dawn
When I shall wake to make him his breakfast
Then sit with eyes dewy, his bath now drawn

The love a young girl feels is not of rue
Her dreams of boys as men suffice as true

I Can Hardly Contain My Glee

I can hardly contain my glee, such joy
He is coming home from college I'm told
Will he call me; oh I hope he's not coy
And sits at home by phone, ardor now cold

The ideas I have garnered I hope they please
The dances, picnics, walk in the park, much more
I've planned; I hope they are not too of ease
And bores him so; boys want something to soar

My friend Alice, she says I should cool it
By that she means let old nature set course
But I'm excited, who else would he visit
I'll go to the station, his train my source

The next day quite early she met his train
He steps off, his arm around a girl, oh pain

Third Section

EOC Office

Struggling, she told me; it wasn't her fault
She was raising two kids alone; no dad
Her job; Police Officer; with that she dealt
Damned good one too and of that she was glad

I asked, what made her ask for my help now
She looked at me; starring, her eyes now tame
I thought, she'll leave, but then her head dropped low
A soft, almost pleading; I'm not to blame

The job pressure, wanting her for night shift
Someone had said she wasn't pulling her load
I asked who; she said the guys were miffed
She shouldn't work days only; umbrage it bode

You are aware this might cause you more grief
But I will file complaint, ask for relief

Then They Deny This Too

There is little time left; her state forlorn
I could almost feel the pathos, the same
Then she began to cry, soft mewls were born
Her whole body shaking like when chills came

I asked if she wanted some clothes, garments
She shook her head, then quite manly, virile
Her eyes aflame, the look of past torments
Began to talk of this cruel, harsh penal

Of the beatings, the rapes; oh yes, they did
Such were these men of God, their taunts worldly
And the rations; moldy breads, the greens wilted
Meat that stank of rotten, the rest wormly

They will kill me now, you know that don't you
Press, you're let in; then they deny this too

Nine Out of Ten

Do you feel me thinking about you now
Do those neurons flashing away give sign
Just a sensate or some prickling allow
Like when dark out walking some ones behind

I will wager we send signals tacit
Have you ever come up short before a gate
Like there was a message saying stop it
And when you did it was the right mandate

When you ponder and the answer pops out
Or an idea to solve a problem appears
Do you take full credit, never have doubt
But then later your spouse's answer mirrors

Take this advice that on hearing a voice
Nine out of ten it will be the right choice

Were You Spying On Me

Last night I walked by your bedroom window
The shades were pulled but light outlined a shape
It was not you but a man's hat bestow
When the light was turned off I stood agape

Were you spying on me, how dare you be
My life is not yours to concern or know
I could have you arrested, a crime you see
So stay away, you're not ever my beau

I see clearly now that I have misjudged
You're a common coquette of loose morals
So good riddance, your love no more be nudged
I'll tell my friends only there were quarrels

Later that day she complained to her mother
I want my old room, the one with boarder

A Girl Bonnie, a Skirt

Have I forsook you for another younger
Tis my shame to do so for you're barren
And the court now wants proof, an heir born here
You'll still be Queen, my love remains no end

To sire a son I have tried most often
But now after five long years there's no child
I have a French cousin of age there in
She will arrive next week, nothing beguiled

To my sister I write of most deceit
My lord will take a young slut to his bed
He tires of me, no love I've known complete
I fear my doom; to the Tower I'm led

Many a lass might ask are I worth dirt
All a man's needs, a girl bonnie, a skirt

Awake I'll Try

She was caught, her daydreams betrayed her now
Send for the guards, remove her to prison
This can't happen she thought how they can know
My dreams are most secret, they're my vision

Silly girl you'll never learn the lesson
If you sit there dreaming; now pay steadfast
Your pen to this paper, thus use reason
For your answer will pass or fail last

There lock the door, make sure no one sees her
She heard the bolt go shut, I'm lost she cried
Sh...the mouse spoke, I'll get you out of here
stay calm, don't fret, when asked answer I lied

What was that my dear, it sounded like I
Oh please give me more time, awake I'll try

I Am But Girl, Pampered

My heart doth pine, it wastes away longing
If I'd only had the courage to speak
To let knownst my ardor, decry wronging
But it would be censored, never to leak

I must wait with patience my needs not heard
A match arranged, I sense bathos instead
Oh to be born again, a son inferred
Happy then I can speak of love as read

I am but girl, pampered, that much is good
And with marriage that still exists for me
Wanton love I feel, oh but if I could
Be then equal in the choosing of thee

Sasha come now for our mealtimes is here
And for your tenth birthday a cake my dear

It's Called Dancing

It's called dancing, listen to the beat sound
Hear it dad, watch me twirl, are you glancing
It's in the air, surrounds tightly the wound
Then spins me out on my tip-toes prancing

And my partners really trying you see
He too feels the music of the airplanes
Their noise deafens so these ear muffs needy
But I still hear the zooms and cracks made pains

Will you take me someday to a ballet
I love the toes when the girls are pointing
But they look quite funny when toes flat lay
Do you think that Swan Lake might be my thing

But in the stead I'll keep up my practice
Letting me feel rhythm in the air entice

Springs a Popping

Springs a popping, I can almost feel it
There's wind of course, it wouldn't be spring without
And the water dishes for birds don't freeze shut
I had better start, prepare bird food throughout

Really, springtime is quite mischief in ways
Some years peaceful, tranquil, almost but then
Wild, late storms; El Niño blamed for delays
All-in-all springs a time you can't depend

I would wish more rainfall but the monsoon
It doesn't come (if at all) till late summer
By that time my flowers grown and missed boon
Without some kind moisture springs a bummer

Each year, now near twenty, I've prayed for rain
Perhaps someone trades for heat, I'd be fain

The Wind to Blow

A cool and fresh blowing, the wind howling
Spring is fighting back with fury against change
But it will lose as Earth revolves rolling
Around the sun, ever it seeks south range

We have no say in our season's going
The Earth's kilter and day spinning ensure
For how dull the weather always knowing
Where the cold spots are and whereby endure

This slant from Earth's axis was a welcome
It not only drives seasons, but the Gulf Stream
This warm ocean water transports heat from
The south to the northern oceans extreme

The Earth's physics are but simple to know
Thus the effects allow the wind to blow

I Write of Spring

I write of spring knowing from whence she came
Like dew drops that wet soft, gently her soles
Of each seed and bud her caress became
The start of growth now wakes from long slept colds

Hard fought sometimes, winter's snares catch her feet
And new growth is stunted or killed outright
But that happens seldom and spring entreat
With lush bounties of new foliage to sight

Spring deals, nay she pesters Thor for her rains
Thor not used to female commands counters
Sends hail, sleet, fog, thunder, what else he feigns
She wears him down, outbursts lessen, flounders

So she rests till summer's lad comes along
Her job fulfilled, amply given now anon

Spring Freeze

It snuck in here, caught some people off guard
A warm spring like week with temp near eighty
Buds were coming out in berry trees hard
And then it struck, the late freeze was mighty

The tree blossoms withered and fell to earth
Early flowers with white candy like frost
Soon died, their life moisture returned to birth
Of course pipes froze then burst when warmed; all lost

Those old timers chuckled, they knew before
Kills the insects so new growth will survive
And they were right, in weeks all would restore
Plumbers complained, imagine that, work derive

Every year the same question in March occurs
Should I plant now or wait till last freeze burrs

Think of Resort

There's a soft breeze blowing, I can feel it
It's dry, always the same each spring coming
There'll be frontal passage soon too I bet
Then on morrow the dust begins scourging

Only good thing about the wind, no bugs
Skeeters can't hatch, there's no standing water
Save some no-see-ums, they hide in your rugs
Put out platter of beer, watch them gather

Soon, well really not fast enough comes summer
This year God may give us monsoons of worth
He's skimped on us a while, a real bummer
The whole southwest is in drought, no rain pour'th

People ask me why live in the desert
When you're thirty below think of resort

Recall the Snow Falling

Recall the snow falling, it was Christmas
Gaily the strung colored lights lit did glow
No tracks, the roads rivers of white fluffed doss
Footprints of two walking, drifting winds blow

Their hands holding, puffs of frost each making
Bundled warm and happy, their cheeks rosy
No words did each utter; pant cuffs caking
Nescient of cold, both now trundled cozy

Stomping their feet outside before entry
Then in stocking feet race quickly inside
Mugs of cocoa and milk from the pantry
Taken with some sugared cookies abide

Pleasures of youth; keepsakes now my daydreams
Wishing I might relive those years of teems

My Roses Grown in Pots

Sniffing the Rose brought back such sweet aroma
Breathing in with huge gulps nearly I swooned
Thereby sitting, pondered the leaf's stoma
Does it too then enjoy the smell thus booned

Leaves so dainty, their shine reflects color
But the Rose is Queenly, mere pawns each leaf
With sharp lancets they guard her with valor
Even with my careful hand a prick brings grief

I will sprinkle Rose food that is au fait
Along with cool water; deserts are dry
They'll bloom from spring to fall, that is if fit
For with Aphids, which sap the juice they die

My Roses grown in pots, I have more success
Perhaps my soil has pests' unknownst I'd guess

White Ribbons

They're white ribbons streaming across the sky
Outlined by blue they grow then fade away
I will follow them, the silver speck high
Travel to those foreign spots now held sway

At times I long; never to see but void
Days, weeks perhaps even months pass on by
Has the silver speck quit, does it avoid
Being without ribbon now hides from eye

Then one bright day they are all there again
I look, straining, the sun overhead, eyes sore
Suppose I should look through field glasses, but then
It wouldn't be a secret to me anymore

Don't you recall as a youngster naming
The cloud figures floating, surely gaming

So Much Out There

We watched the moon rising, my son and I
Like a silver disc, it looked much larger
A trick someone said; just looks to the eye
They could fool me, novice gazers I'd wager

Because of the moonlight we saw the brightest
Venus and Mars were there too; no Saturn
Orion, we saw the belt but the rest hidest
Over our heads the Big Dipper we learn

We talked of the vastness of space explore
Was our flag still planted, the Moon's dusty
And the probes that brought us pictures galore
We're the robot lunar rovers rusty

So much out there; little of it we've seen
Like our thoughts still quiet, someday to glean

Nature's Gambles

There is a spot I seek not far away
Of rocks helter-skelter, placed there through luck
And in between grows green of grass and Bay
My own jumble, a world of nips and tuck

I sat nearby, watching for some movement
And then scurried a small lizard tail high
He looked towards me, his legs pumping, intent
Was he thinking, is that danger I spy

In a dark hole appeared what I'd hoped for
Cougar kittens, orange balls of fur peeking
I had hidden so not to spook them more
I watched until back in the hole, napping

Just think of all those spots where you can sit
And watch nature's gambles of kit and wit

A Place Special

Over yonder there is a place special
Cold, clear water taps from mountain's storage
Into a pool, deep dug, there swims docile
Mama Cougar, searching the pools selvage

When she departs, Mule Deer come to refresh
Long ears turning, listening, always watchful
They will depart quickly if sound is harsh
But for today they drink quick each mouthful

At dusk, the White Wing Doves come in flapping
They drink before nesting in dense foliage
Then in darkness the wee critters lapping
Always aware that Owl lurks near, most sage

This place survives because it is hidden
And that Congress in years now past bidden

Brown Eyes Saw Him

Oft in the mist he thought, a sound was heard
There now, again, but the sound now softened
He made his way, careful of low branches jarred
Again the soft sound made, now close to end

In a low spot the mist lifting, a form
It lay amid leaves and wet bramble of Rose
Slowly he walked, not sure, would there be harm
Bending down now it looked like a dog, close

Brown eyes saw him, he thought pleading for help
It now appeared the dog had been shot once
His seen grievous wound crippling now this whelp
Assessing the shots damage; lifted, heard grunts

On his car's front floor he laid the young pet
Covered with his coat he sped for the vet

I've Missed All the Pursuits

When I'm asleep and all is still inside
When calm is wind, evenings darkness covers
The night creatures venture forth from their hide
With soft flutters, bats zig-zagging gathers

Stealth the feral Cat knows, he's learned it well
A mouse or vole, perhaps a dead bird found
The Jack Rabbit watches the Cat, his ears still
Both fear Coyote running in groups, noses down

The night's silent stalker hoot, hoots his call
Death floats quickly, his sharp talons grab best
A loud shriek, then quiet, a kill that's all
Labored flapping, the Owl returns to nest

When I awake next morn and greet the day
I've missed all the pursuits, gambits or play

I'm Here to Love You

Would that I could hold you, slumber my nest
There spoon like your body warm and content
My arms around, your sweet perfume caressed
I am drunken with love, this night's portent

Then to hear your soft mews whispered the air
And with gentle squeezes your breath catching
I turn you towards me, your brown eyes aware
Then those red lips accept mine now matching

Our kisses explore there each crevice with tongue
The touch and play, tagging you have me best
As my ardor increases pressure my lung
Awake I find my cat upon my chest

Twinkie licks my nose, she senses my anguish
I'm here to love you, her eyes make that wish

Fourth Section

This Sets the Stage

Picture in time of the Bard of Avon
William Shakespeare's era, late sixteen hundreds
A small village with some bridgework upon
Sat a pub called Wild Boar known for its suds

On one such night then sat a pair drinking
One of noble bearing called by young sir
His mate in tow called Will, sat numb blinking
Both had drank past limits on fine liquor

Nearly closing, young sir got up most bold
'Twas the later assumed he left for home
Friend Will far from sober passed out cold
When the barkeep locked up he heard Will moan

This sets the stage; let all be knownst the plight
For our young sir begins his geste this night

Drink Not the Wine of Love

Gently repose you of whispers spoken
Let your body lie in moss laid nesting
While the Fairies fan their wings in token
Cool breeze so blown across where you're resting

Out of hearing the Sprites purling enchant
They speak of love taken by you tonight
With blush, intone ardor viewed so gallant
They soon depart in pairs this place in flight

As dawn sneaks in the Fairies awaken hover
Amid chatter you rise to greet what may
Be still, you say, how come here, I aver
With much giggles and mirth relate my story

I thus impart wisdom for you, young males
Drink not the wine of love, else, be of tales

My Wisdom Not Taken

Tell me great sir, where for you went last night
Your pals, include humble servant, know not
The last we saw, of wine partake; you tight
You then stumbled out from Wild Boar a sot

We searched till light; Will here, trotted canal
Nary a sight; so tell us now your tale
I then did speak; not sir, falsehoods, but all
Warning, after I spoke, partake less ale

Of what manner this tale freely buccal
You think us louts, who drink here most nightly
Be oft then rogue, no more imbibe local
We're done; barman, show him the door rightly

Outside, I swore; cast me the devil to friends
I'll search thru hills and vales, for fair play ends

Not All Is Trickery of Knave

I've set to search for those Fairies and Sprites
That has caused much laughter and shame to me
I have my sword and stick to blow in fights
And should I be stricken, siffle for tea

And by the river in a thicket I spy
The same that took me here bumbling that night
Stay, I command, be not oft for I spry
And catch of you, batter with all my might

Please Sir, strike not my Sprites for I implore
You hear of the alleged grievous affair
For on that night my Sprites found you most sore
Bleeding, you were taken here and made fair

For you see not all is trickery of knave
My Sprites and winged Fairies of you, did save

CALL THIS NONSENSE

My minds bemused with these melodies most faire
Do these Fairies use wile; entice like me
I am besot; stumble I to their lair
Confused, my eyes will not focus rightly

An Elf, action winsome, approaches towards
Kind sir, you have wandered into our nest
We have, you will notice, bewitched all bards
As your poems do entreat humans infest

Tonight we will revel, with you our guest
So join in our festive and make merry
Then let Fairies carry you to fond rest
At dawn, no thoughts remain, so don't tarry

I've tried now to explain my eve's absence
But my drinking chaps laugh, call this nonsense

Flinging Kisses

What speak young Sir; you wish follow and see
To roust this den, as you say now harbors
And you offer, a fresh tipping of tea
Fairies; be off, go seek yonder arbors

I plead my case, there are Spirits most true
How else convince but by thy own eye sight
If we fail, then promise I will to you
No more I'll say of Elves and Sprites to night

What say my lads, should we follow as cur
Or throw him in canal, that'll cool his boast
I say give him his due, I'll join young Sir
Another; that makes now three which march on soused

Townsmen would say later to their misses
We saw the three marching, flinging kisses

Grievous Harm Doth Appear

I spoke to my friends dear; Will and Jeffrey
Let us not speak except in hush whispers
Prove all we're not batty in the belfry
Poor chance convince those souls now at vespers

We crept along the fens, then to treed dells
Motioned to my cohorts to walk slowly
I spied a Sprite, signaled a halt; more Elves
We lay down in wetness, our breathes brumous

Soon more Fairies joined the summoned gather
Cold, we quivered so much a noise of rustle
And now disclosed, the Sprites in a lather
We're bound and mouths muffled; now all bustle

Young Sir, we warned of bards seeking us here
And with two sots, grievous harm doth appear

Three Scant-O-Grace

I then motioned, as was unable to talk
The lead Elf took pity removed my gag
Speak bard or I'll replace, your voice not walk
Oh your Honor, please Sir we meant no rag

Compeers Will and Jeffrey did not lead here
I ask remove their binds, let us succor
We'll not tell of concourse, no more you'll fear
Our friends we'll tell of prank, for your rapport

Your plea I do accept, but all must swear
That on mid-night no more explores our haunt
Of that all three did swear, then bade leave lair
The walks back home no words or yell, as daunt

There was tell of three scant-o-grace drinking
Their faces showing wonder, some said thinking

Beer to All that Came

Good Sprites tell my Fairies it's time to leave
Those brash humans, they'll not relent to spy
Thus we'll go to Ireland, its green believe
Those folks a more gentle kind I espy

But Queen do we leave here, never return
Our nests and the English flowers we'll miss
Silence, we are leaving, Eire you'll learn
And dance the jig, the stout Irish our wish

And so they moved, twas told a swarm was seen
But that was said a flock of birds or ducks
And in a vale ran cool water there been
A slight tempest in a teapot amid yucks

The fine Irish wishing welcome proclaim
Elfin's Day which means beer to all that came

By Ship from Port, Forthwith

Hail young Sir, come join our table, pray do
Bar keep draw ale, put it on my bill
I did then sit and ease became me through
For ne'er a man so fine as this my Will

Then did Jeffrey join our group now four
The pubs owner, a man named Scott sat with
So tell me said Scott, how propose this tour
I then answered, by ship from port forthwith

Our ship left Cardiff bound for Dublin
Twas a splendid sail, the sea fresh with wind
By late afternoon we docked and made way in
I had booked rooms at the Brazen Head Inn

That eve we sat and smoked; Irish ale sipped
A long day for me, then good nights so lipped

Along River Liffey

This inn could use me; needs repair, said Scott
So it should, it's older than our England
Not as old as this brew, drink up you sot
Where to young sir, a tour of faire Ireland

Leaving Dublin we then explored inland
Along River Liffey (it means A Life)
We walked and soon tired, Scott had brought food grand
Will praised; barkeeps know but did you pack knife

Surfeit, all were sleepy and soon be napped
As their snores and short grunts went on in sleep
A Sprite flew close, surveyed the group now sapped
Then it returned, telling of find it'd reap

The Queen of Elves pondered what she'd been told
This group, you say of three be knownst of old

About Sprites Thick

Arouse ye, let us be off for time passes quick
And we have a distance to go today
I had a dream, said Scott, about Sprites thick
They lay in fact waiting along our way

You're as bad as young Sir, Will spoke chiding
Telling of Elves, Sprites and Fairies about
Well it was a vivid dream worth citing
And we do not know these paths here without

I say we should return to inn forthwith
Follow close the river back to Dublin
We can ask the inn keep about elves myth
And I could use a stout ale, thirst buildin'

As the quartet walked back they were noisy
The Queen wondered, would they now bring posse

Trouble She Feared

We must inquest, get the people to look
But Scott we were given precept to stop
The three of us promised, our vow she took
To bring others will just seem like a sop

No Scott we mustn't alarm any Irish
The Sprites, Fairies will keep distance from town
I'll take Will here, explore river for fish
We'll not menace their lair, safety thus shown

So Will and I ventured up the river
In a cool spot resting the Queen appeared
At once I spoke, told of promise we aver
Elf Queen halted my speak, trouble she feared

We heard concern, it was redoubt being
Seems they bivouacked too close, Irish Elfs seeing

Pardons Given

Here is my plan Queen Elf, approve I pray
Let us invade the band you called Irish
Pester them as we done before with lay
Made most unrhymed; soon they depart our wish

Then with Will, Scott, Jeffrey and me we're off
And soon they are spotted camped as Queen told
With hoot and much holler we played drunk toff
Falling often, then in loud voices yelled bold

Then the Elfin band on hearing noise there
Made haste their own retreat telling of woe
Let us go to Galway, leave this roister
We can sit by the bay, watch old men row

All were joyous then with much back slapping
Pardons given, the Queen bade them clapping

While Away, Grow Old

We left young sir's party absolved by Elf
Thus they returned once more to fair Dublin
There made plans to return home, pleased with self
But Scott lingered behind his mind muddling

I've been thinking he then announced to all
This town is in need of another tavern
I'll thus stay here, build pub, Elves Tale my ale
So the threesome set sail, thence their return

Will jumped to the quay, his manner happy
But young sir and Jeffrey waited resigned
Make haste you two; we're for the pub snappy
I'll buy the first round, our posture defined

The brave trio will while away, grow old
Perhaps this tale is now finished; well told

Puck's Drops

Come; let me put Puck's drops into her eyes
For when she wakes, then glances perchance my face
And full in rapture takes in loves surprise
That my visage be her first to embrace

I thus copy of Bard, his play a farce
Whilst not middle summer I hoped for best
I took my friend Charles with in tow of course
My plan, we'd meet en route, set forth the test

At eight she came, my heart beating rapid
I then motioned Charles to lie back, turning
There, that's good as...I felt a bump...stupid
I fell face down, she passed, saw Charles, yearning

Often I've paused, pondered what went wrongful
Blaming Shakespeare, why that is just spiteful

I Have Often Dreamt

I have often dreamt at starry night time
That time between dusk and dawn when quiet falls
And hushes heard, sweet nothings tumbling in rhyme
Where dark shadowed forms dance around the walls

That I join with Fairies gathered near me
Their wings beating swiftly, the hum like bees
Where do we go I ask, some place near be
Nay, they say, far away before Sprites tease

Then with a flash we soar like a comet
Towards the Big Bear above in the heavens
Looking back at Earth I sense the moment
Such blues, greens, browns, along with whites at ends

I feel giddy falling freely towards Earth
Till when softly I float back into my birth

Such of Foolish Talk

Oh my Séarlait [SHER let] I wish I was Etaoin [Ay deen]
To be of such beauty, be in total
The love of two Kings and I could be Queen
Midir of the Fairies; Airem, mortal

Màiréad [MAY rayd], my child you should not so daydream
Your life is to serve your father, our Lord
And he has now chosen a man, Brésnainn [BREH-neen]
You do well to obey, to make afford

Yet I do so dream of love that's not loss
To be wooed and given flowers of scent
Then with him to sail the ocean across
To gain as their Queen by my prince there sent

Such of foolish talk, let me draw your bath
And best you shall forget least this bring wrath

Fairy King – Midir
Mortal King – Airem
Princess – Màiréad
Lady in waiting = Séarlait
Goddess of Beauty and wooed by Midir and Airem – Etaoin

Tant Pis Mortals

When dew drops form and night settles the din
Then the Fairies dance and play with much glee
And Sprites finesse honey off Bees therein
The Elves hold court, there's much furore to be

Strangers, not the locals have been seen near
They are most quite outré observed by Sprites
Trampling flowers and with nets causes much fear
Enough cries their Queen, seek and proclaim our rights

At dawn Fairies and Sprites set out en masse
Their plan to cause mischief, hinder their joy
They changed the path, poisoned Oak they will pass
Watching they saw much of alarm their ploy

As the sun sets flowers closed their petals
Peace and quiet returned tant pis mortals

[tant pis means too bad]

My Tears Fall Tonight

My sweet darling, tonight of love I write
Hoping when you read this I shall live fair
And then soon to your arms holding me tight
Never to leave again, this my oath swear

But in honest words I fear most greatly
That I shall not survive open volley
The line of men, my own command; firstly
Truly brave these men are, but such folly

I want you to recall our times merry
To hold them dear always in your bosom
Still you are young, so should you then marry
Pick a fellow my age, with him blossom

I do so love you, my tears fall tonight
Then at dawn, with my sword drawn we will fight

I Hope I Write More Soon

Dear Ma, I write this note as I am told
At the break of day we eat our ration
Then check our gear, drink coffee, its cold
Muster soon then after we march station

Our young Captain has told us we are brave
He has a girl back home, hopes to marry
I told him of Kelly, I guess I rave
You'll tell her Ma, should God then me carry

Tell my brother he can have my banjo
My dog, Sam I give to young Bess to own
All the rest you can have, I leave it so
John Brown from the valley has saw on loan

I miss you Ma, I hope I write more soon
But on morrow we face our foes platoon

Ryback Captured

Mary dear the mail arrived, there's a letter
Is it from my Captain Ryback; from Joe
No dear it's from Major Adams; sit here
Why are you not letting me read...Oh no

Here dear, do you wish to read it yourself
Mother is Joe dead, tell me, you've heard
Major Adams writes of your Joe himself
Says that many died, but Ryback captured

Captured; does that mean he's alive and well
No dear, it means only that he's taken
We must wait and pray, there now, do not dwell
I will write to father; queries be spoken

Mary you must rest now, take care darling
There may be news later; parley going

Makes Little Matter Who Won

Dear Ma, God must watch that I am not killed
Oh, the fighting was so gruesome around
I must have shot maybe ten rounds, some skilled
We pushed them back, we stood, controlled our ground

Captain Ryback bravely led our first charge
I was told then by some he had been shot
But our Major says he was seen at large
Later we were told of capture the lot

For my actions I have now been cited
That's what Major Adams said, it's given
I will have my own squad, eight righted
That means more pay, better my life liven

All here wish this fight be over and done
To me it makes little matter who won

Jack, That's Me You-all

Dear Ma; today was a good one; pray Jack
My squad patrolled beyond the field's battle
Saw where they had taken Captain Ryback
Some men wanted to go follow, rattle

I said you can rattle game, not our foes
Besides, eight men are not enough to engage
On the return we did capture stragglers
Maybe then we can learn from their visage

Major Adams said one had proved useful
He gave location where the captives were held
Told all Company that Jack, that's me you-all
Would be ranked as Sergeant; that's done in field

I now command the 8th Platoon, some job
There's no officers here now, Ryback's new fob

Our Raid Covert

Listen up men, one that we took captive
He's spilled where our Captain Ryback is held
About half hour horse ride; men get active
We go at dusk, our raid covert, thus veiled

We stopped a mile short, all would sneak forward
Using my hand signaled don't fire your gun
Then we saw camp, few guards posted inward
Our plan surprise, then grab our prize and run

I said go and we were running full speed
The guards caught lax, little defense they made
Gotten the key opened the cage and freed
Saw the Captain was weak so grabbed to aid

Back at camp I wrote of rescue to mom
Captain Ryback's wedding; I'm asked to come

About the Author

Stanley Thompson wrote his first poems over fifty years ago while at college. Following the death of his wife in 2011 he restarted his writing of poetry. His background is impressive and shows the array of interests and accomplishments that have allowed him to write on a variety of subjects. In addition he has traveled extensively throughout the world gaining insight of the peoples he writes about.

A retired Naval Officer and pilot of carrier jet aircraft he also received his Masters degree in Meteorology at the U. S. Naval Postgraduate School. He has taught college level mathematics, statistics, oceanography and naval history courses in four separate universities. He was comptroller and later president of an aviation company. He has held senior management positions in a long-term Adolescent Psychiatric Hospital. This was followed with many years of search and rescue duties for the St. Louis County Sheriff in Minnesota and later as a patrol deputy in Sierra County of New Mexico.

His extensive voluntary service includes Chairman of a District Hospital; Township Supervisor; Chairman of the Local Emergency Preparedness Committee, and Lt. Colonel in the New Mexico State Defense Force. He continues his life writing on average three poems per day, volunteering at a church food shelf weekly and singing in choruses and his church choir.

Mr. Thompson resides in Southern New Mexico with his cat named Twinkle Toes or as he affectionately refers, "Twinkie", a pet Rattlesnake called Floyd which roams freely, and countless Quail, Dove and birds with occasional Coyotes thrown in.

www.ingramcontent.com/pod-product-compliance
Lightning Source LLC
Chambersburg PA
CBHW030937090426
42737CB00007B/457